ENDORSEMENT FOR

Sonnets for the Soul

A wonderful devotional created by a Christian Life Coach that will lift your spirit in a creative new way.
—**W. Drain**

An inspiring devotional, contemplative but easy to read and helps you see yourself through God's eyes.
—**M. Hacker**

I couldn't imagine buying a book of poetry until I saw a snippet of this one. You will be very inspired and also learn a lot from a great Christian Life Coach.
—**Y. Singh**

Inspiring and powerful devotional you should give as a gift. You will want your co-workers,

neighbors, friends, and family to experience the uplifting messages in each poem.
—**J. Bare**

Well written and highly insightful!
—**L. Niess**

This is a wonderful devotional of poems. LtA has truly been filled with God's Grace.
—**B. Estrada**

LtA delivers the gospel in a beautiful way. You can tell how much LtA love's the Lord and this devotional will overwhelm your heart as you read how He has written on LtA's heart in order to assemble each poem.
—**Dorothy**

Sonnets For the Soul:

31 Inspiring Sonnets for Daily Christian Living
Volume I

CHRISTIAN LIFE COACHING

By LtA

Published by Kharis Publishing, imprint of Kharis Media LLC.

Copyright © 2020 by LtA

ISBN-13: 978-1-946277-90-9

ISBN-10: 1-946277-90-8

Library of Congress Control Number: 2020950649

Cover image: Pexels/Steve Johnson

All rights reserved. This book or parts thereof may not be reproduced in any form, stored in a retrieval system, or transmitted in any form by any means - electronic, mechanical, photocopy, recording, or otherwise - without prior written permission of the publisher, except as provided by United States of America copyright law.

Scripture quotations marked (NIV) are taken from the Holy Bible, New International Version®, NIV®. Copyright © 1973, 1978, 1984, 2011 by Biblica, Inc.™ Used by permission of Zondervan. All rights reserved worldwide. www.zondervan.com The "NIV" and "New International Version" are trademarks registered in the United States Patent and Trademark Office by Biblica, Inc.™

Scripture quotations marked (NKJV) Scripture taken from the New King James Version. Copyright © 1982 by Thomas Nelson, Inc. Used by permission. All rights reserved.

Scripture quotations marked (ESV) The ESV Global Study Bible®, ESV® Bible
Copyright © 2012 by Crossway. All rights reserved. The Holy Bible, English Standard Version® (ESV®) Copyright © 2001 by

Sonnet for the Soul

Crossway, a publishing ministry of Good News Publishers. All rights reserved. ESV Text Edition: 2016

Scripture quotations marked (NLT) *Holy Bible*, New Living Translation, copyright © 1996, 2004, 2015 by Tyndale House Foundation. Used by permission of Tyndale House Publishers, Inc., Carol Stream, Illinois 60188. All rights reserved.

Scripture quotations marked TPT are from The Passion Translation® Copyright © 2017, 2018 by Passion & Fire Ministries, Inc. Used by permission. All rights reserved. ThePassionTranslation.com.

All KHARIS PUBLISHING products are available at special quantity discounts for bulk purchase for sales promotions, premiums, fund-raising, and educational needs. For details, contact:

Kharis Media LLC
Tel: 1-479-599-8657
<u>support@kharispublishing.com</u>

DEDICATION

Thank you to my family who encouraged me and supported me to step outside my comfort zone to write this book of poetry.

Thank you to my spouse, without you, none of this is possible.

Believers have a lot to offer in His name. We can be transformed by the power of His Word while enjoying our journey with Christ. See yourself the way God sees you, not the way the enemy describes you. When you choose to lay your foundation on the Word of God, you will be able to withstand what the enemy throws at you and come out on the other side intact and stronger than ever.

Thank you to all the readers who love the Word as much as I do!

CONTENTS

Preface	ix
Introduction	xi
Sonnets Devotional	1
Conclusions	127
About the Author	130

PREFACE

Whatever burdens you carried into this sonnet devotional reading; I pray you lay them at His feet.

> *For the commandment is a lamp,*
> *And the law a light;*
> *Reproofs of instruction are the way of life*
> Proverbs 6:23 | NKJV

I define poetry as an effort to share a moving experience by using language that is chosen and structured differently from the ordinary writing style.

Using words differently from an ordinary writing style is a poet's way of trying to awaken something in not only the poet's experience, but perhaps also in the reader's experience.

Because we have the ability to understand and appreciate various forms of literature, God used many genres to communicate His Word.

For this devotional, I have chosen to use the English sonnet style of poetry as this book's schematic. Each sonnet has been inspired by the stirring of the Holy Spirit. I pray my maiden journey into this expression of writing, which strays from the strictest of sonnet practices from time to time, will bless you and help draw you closer to the Lord.

Let's begin…

For more information on the author and this book please visit:

ChristianLifeCoachingbyLtA.com

Facebook
Twitter
Instagram
Pinterest
LinkedIn

Introduction

God Speaks through Poems. Jesus is one of the most famous poets of the world.

Approximately one-third of the Bible is poetic. Whole books of the Bible are poetic: Job, Psalms, Proverbs, Song of Solomon. A majority of Old Testament prophecy is poetic in form. Beyond these predominantly poetic parts of the Bible, figurative language appears throughout the Word; and whenever it does, it requires the same type of analysis given to poetry.

That is a lot of poetry. God can raise the dead by any means He pleases. He can waken dull hearts to the reality of His beauty any way He desires. And one of the ways He pleases to do it is by inspiring His spokesmen to write poetry.

Contemplative communication is not popular. We do not live in a day when poetry is in Vogue. A world shaped by smartphones and soundbites, we are impatient with communication that forces us to slow down.

God filled the Bible with all kinds of writing besides poetry. He knows that some people prefer stories, like in the Gospels. Others prefer arguments, like in Romans. So, I will understand if you are not a poetry-lover. But don't limit yourself too quickly. People change. Times change.

This may be the season for you to slow down and reconsider.

Please use the following sonnet devotional to help grow your spiritual pantry—reflect, ponder, and increase your intimacy with Christ!

God bless,

LtA

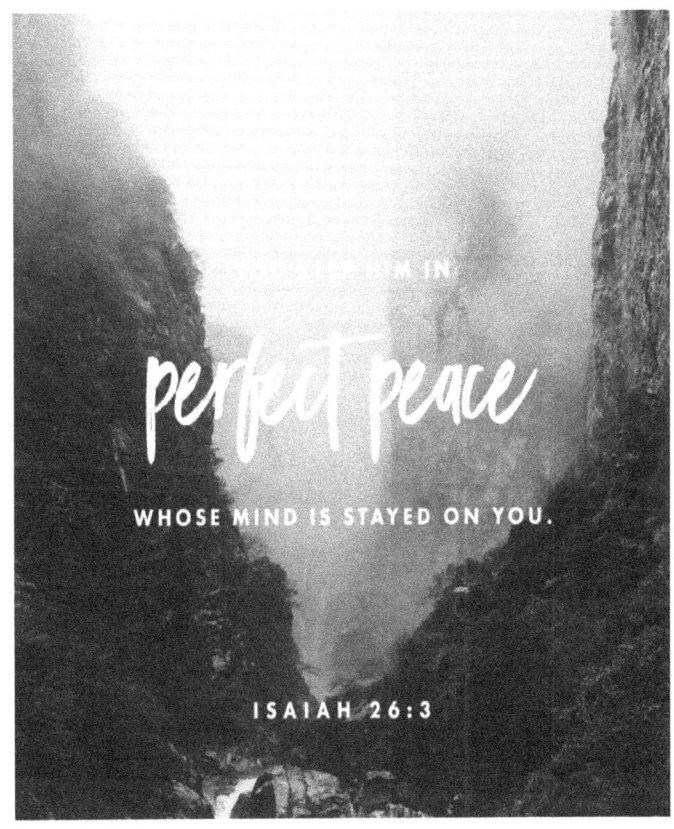

*You will show me the path of life;
In Your presence is fullness of joy;
At Your right hand are pleasures
forevermore.*

Psalm 16:11 | NKJV

Journey Through

I need the Holy Spirit to guide the *path*.
In Your HANDS are PLEASURES for all of **Yours**.
There is no doubt I would endure Your *wrath*,
therefore, I must enter through the grace **doors**.

Now how to receive your FULLNESS of **joy?**
It is never Your will for me to *fail*,
Holy Spirit please reveal the **decoy**,
it's by Your HAND alone I will *prevail*.

The veil torn, separated **nevermore**.
Apposed to all those whom sow harvest in *strife*,
the enemy's scheme banished **forevermore**,
by Your provision, have abundant *life*.

In Your PRESENCE I'm refreshed, filled with **shine**,
now I am overflowing within the **Divine**.

LHA

Notes:

All that the Father gives me will come to me, and whoever comes to me I will never cast out.

John 6:37 | ESV

Ceaseless Love

The Savior promises you can **measure.**
The enemy's scheme is all to *despair.*
We were all created for His **pleasure.**
Enter My covenant and find *repair.*

I am pleased; in My name, you **labor.**
My plans for you will not keep you *oppressed.*
If you love Me, show love to your **neighbor.**
COME, don't delay, your spirit can find *rest.*

In the past, had the enemy **provoked**?
I will take your worries and all *burden.*
Through repentance and faith, we are **yoked,**
for all are welcome to be *transferred in.*

As promised, you are the head, not the **tail,**
entering into heaven you will **sail.**

Notes:

Yes, I am the vine; you are the branches. Those who remain in me, and I in them, will produce much fruit. For apart from me you can do nothing.

John 15:5 | NLT

Dependence

I lean in to hear a gentle **whisper**.
Now that I am supported by the ***VINE,***
when my head is low, You are the **lifter.**
Your mercy met my sin and I interact with the ***Divine.***

APART from You, I had zero **chances,**
distant, on my own, unable to bear ***FRUIT.***
Your grace never departs, so my **BRANCHES**
one day You will reveal my new white ***suit.***

Remind me the pain of being **pruned**
allows nourishment to improve my ***growth.***
The new FRUIT worth the temporary **wound.**
As You tend to my branch, I cling to ***both.***

Please cultivate, dear VINE and **vinedresser,**
all gifts come from my heavenly **Blesser.**

LHA

Notes:

And the Lord, He is the One who goes before you. He will be with you, He will not leave you nor forsake you; do not fear nor be dismayed.

Deuteronomy 31:8 | NKJV

Let Me Alone

LORD, You promise that even though I've **strayed**
I need not FEAR and can be of good ***cheer.***
DISMAYED You are not, forever You **paid.**
When I need You, faithfully You ***appear.***

FORSAKE, You will not. My heart will not **ache.**
With Your mercy and grace, I will not ***grieve***
You. With mercies anew every **daybreak,**
kneeling at the foot of Your cross I ***cleave.***

New heart in place, in me, Your chosen **home.**
Love You have shown, my heart You have ***captured.***
My flesh wars, please help me to never **roam.**
Certain our bond will never be ***fractured.***

Word speaks life, Father of heavenly lights **be,**
those who mean harm and hide in darkness **flee**!

LHA

Notes:

So now we must cling tightly to the hope that lives within us, knowing that God always keeps his promises!

Hebrews 10:23 | TPT

Hold Fast

The law was given, but HOPE was **misplaced.**
GOD raised a righteous branch, in David's *shoot*
So, His dear children would not be **disgraced.**
For whomever believes shares this deep *root*.

You hung on a cross so I wouldn't feel **shame.**
There was no other way to Your *embrace.*
The enemy wants me to share this **blame.**
Calvary, outside walls was the *place.*

You carried their weapon not **wavering**,
For all who believe are very *grateful.*
New covenant we can be **savoring**.
CLINGING to a God Who is quite *praiseful!*

Your hand in mine, PROMISE to hold it **tight**
as You illuminate a world with **light.**

LHA

Notes:

Be still, and know that I am God.
I will be exalted among the nations,
I will be exalted in the earth!

Psalm 46:10 | ESV

Divine Protector

NATIONS, stop wasting time **monologuing.**
Why do you think I sent My Son to *EARTH?*
I want relationship, start **dialoguing!**
When you seek Him is when you find your *worth.*

EXALTED above all, never **halted.**
With the Cornerstone as your *foundations*
to your sinful nature you **defaulted.**
Your Defender, brought back in *relations.*

My throne, surrounded by angels, a **height**
You can't see. But benefit from the *breadth*
of My love. No time of the day or **night**
will I fail to protect you from the *depth.*

BE STILL, AND KNOW I AM all **around!**
Opponents be gone, for My Son bent **down.**

LHA

Notes:

Come to me, all you who are weary and burdened, and I will give you rest.

Matthew 11:28 | NIV

Relief

Lord, You invite me to receive Your **REST**.
Both body and spirit I am ***stressed***.
We've begun our journey and in my **quest**,
You embrace me and I become ***refreshed***.

When the clouds arrive and darken and **form**,
when I am WEARY, You give perfect ***peace***.
As this journey of life will bring a **storm**,
Lord, You promise my BURDEN will ***decease***.

The groans of my growing pains show **strength**.
This captive You set free is now feeling ***glee***,
restoring my faith to such a great **length**.
You are the Way, and to You I bend ***knee***.

Lord, the world is in need of **revival**.
Instead we're taught it's about **survival**.

LtA

Notes:

Since we are receiving a Kingdom that is unshakable, let us be thankful and please God by worshiping him with holy fear and awe.

Hebrews 12:28 | NLT

Throne of Grace

Jesus, because You came to save and **bled,**
I WORSHIP and praise You with a THANKFUL
heart.
Grasping Your HOLY seamless garment's **thread**,
RECEIVING a KINGDOM where we don't ***part.***

Now finding security in Your **blood,**
all mankind can be spared by Your ***mercy.***
I enjoy the new covenant post **flood,**
walking by faith, there is no ***controversy.***

When I thirst and life is too much to **bear,**
and when my heart is unable to ***take,***
in AWE I reflect on the me You choose to **spare.**
Please God remind me that I do not ***break.***

In Your grace it is **unmistakable,**
Because of You I am **UNSHAKEABLE**.

Notes:

*By your patience possess
your souls.*

Luke 21:19 | NKJV

Endureth

Teacher, although life can sting with **trials**,
You inwardly renew; I will not ***yield***.
Your kindness for me stretches for **miles**.
Seated on high, undefeated, my ***shield***.

Your life, my gain; gloriously **appearing**.
The enemy says it's too much to ***bear***,
You dwell in me, I am **persevering**.
The pain of Your cross I willingly ***share***.

The chains broken, to the end I **endure**.
Without Your grace gift, the way not ***paved***,
Perfector of faith, You are the one **cure**.
Good News for all who in Christ are ***saved***.

I can be PATIENT through my **affliction**,
because You provided the **prescription**.

LHA

Notes:

Purge me with hyssop,

and I shall be clean;

wash me,

and I shall be whiter than snow.

Psalm 51:7 | ESV

Relationship Healed

God, You surprise with the **impossible.**
PURGING and purifying as if to ***CLEAN,***
taking my filthy rags and making them **washable.**
Us, together in pastures, what a ***scene!***

Sinless, You became our sin **sacrifice.**
I could not reach You, held in a ***prison,***
The King of Kings, paid the final debt **price.**
You came to serve and save, now have ***risen.***

When You ascended, You left us Your **peace.**
Deliverance by works, no one ***achieves.***
By this miracle, You have made my **fleece,**
and treasures in heaven, sheltered from ***thieves.***

There's no fear when I hear the trumpet **blow,**
You made me WHITE as SNOW, I'm set ***aglow.***

LtA

Notes:

I have been crucified with Christ. It is no longer I who live, but Christ who lives in me. And the life I now live in the flesh I live by faith in the Son of God, who loved me and gave himself for me.

Galatians 2:20 | ESV

Blended

The Law, unable to make us **upright**.
Spiritual death rose to a new life, *surged*.
Eyes fixed on the cross, new life our **birthright**.
Amongst CHRIST in His CRUCIFIXION, *merged*.

Old on the cross, unfettered from sin's **grip**,
body of sin destroyed, our *advantage*.
Freed from the dominion of guilt we **skip**,
in communion with CHRIST, lead and *manage*.

Dead to the world's allurements and the **snares**.
BY FAITH in CHRIST, we have *intercession*,
and grace for a holy LIFE as His **heirs**.
LOVE furnished redemption through *concession*.

Fountain of LIFE in my soul **internal**,
saved from the anguish of death **eternal**.

Notes:

I have given you authority to trample on snakes and scorpions and to overcome all the power of the enemy; nothing will harm you.

Luke 10:19 | NIV

Preservation

Symbols of POWERS: Pharisees and **scribes,**
defended from peril having no ***debt.***
SCORPIONS, alike wicked men, take **bribes.**
God of grace secures removal of ***threat.***

Promise of victory OVER sin's **sway.**
Victory OVER the baleful we ***boast.***
Victory OVER the devil's **highway.**
Divine POWER reins Satan and his ***hosts.***

Outward miracles shall not **satisfy.**
Temporal favors no longer ***delight.***
Pursuing renovation in the **sky,**
ladders rising to heaven, a ***spotlight.***

Subsisting among the vast **malignant,**
accusations won't leave you **indignant.**

LHA

Notes:

*²² Through the Lord's mercies we are not consumed,
Because His compassions fail not.
²³ They are new every morning;
Great is Your faithfulness.
²⁴ "The Lord is my portion," says my soul,
"Therefore I hope in Him!"*
Lamentations 3:22-24 | NKJV

Dawn of Mercies

Each morning Your loving MERCIES **anew**.
Mighty God, You are FAITHFUL to the *end.*
Not CONSUMED, how many can I **accrue**?
My daily prayer, that I never *blend.*

Your boundless COMPASSIONS, they do not **rust.**
Earthly riches so easy to *destroy.*
Before Your creation returns to **dust,**
Your eternal FAITHFULNESS we *enjoy.*

Your presence is the best **inheritance**.
You are my PORTION, never *perishing*.
Empty inside, remove any **arrogance**.
Confidence in You, I am *cherishing.*

Humbly, into a world You came to **save,**
I need You daily to help me be **brave**.

Notes:

³⁸ And I am convinced that nothing can ever separate us from God's love. Neither death nor life, neither angels nor demons, neither our fears for today nor our worries about tomorrow—not even the powers of hell can separate us from God's love. ³⁹ No power in the sky above or in the earth below—indeed, nothing in all creation will ever be able to separate us from the love of God that is revealed in Christ Jesus our Lord.

Romans 8:38-39 | NLT

Warfare

Because of Your love, I'm a **conqueror.**
From the day You called me, You had my *heart.*
Sanctified, yes. No longer a **wanderer.**
By Your POWER I have been set *apart.*

The battle is real, but no need to **fret.**
In the armor of CHRIST, I am *covered.*
No power ABOVE or BELOW a **threat.**
Past battle wounds healed; I am *recovered.*

Ready to protect and keep, strength and **shield.**
You bought me then. You sealed it with a *price.*
Nothing compares to the glory **REVEALED**.
Your gift to me: eternal *Paradise.*

I'm CONVINCED that NOTHING can **SEPARATE**
us from Your LOVE, not even Satan's **bait.**

LHA

Notes:

*Trust in the Lord and do good;
dwell in the land and enjoy safe
pasture.*

Psalm 37:3 | NIV

Promise of Preservation

Everlasting God, Your Word Is **flawless.**
The unjust appear happy and ***thriving.***
My spirit shouts; in You I find **solace,**
as I await Your second ***arriving.***

Temporarily, wickedness **abounds.**
I am not disturbed, in You I ***confide.***
The day is near when the trumpet will **sound,**
caught up in Your grace, the ultimate ***guide.***

Omnipresent One, You are every **place.**
Thrills of heaven explained, I never ***could.***
I will TRUST in You, as I run this **race**
and I'll stop complaining, instead DO ***GOOD.***

I'll DWELL in Your house, this You **enabled.**
As I lean into You, I'll be **cradled.**

LHA

Notes:

Casting all your anxieties on him, because he cares for you.

1 Peter 5:7 | ESV

In the Lord's Care

Your providence, Lord, I do not **distrust.**
I am part of Your high *society,*
pending the day I will return to **dust.**
Heavenward, I CAST my ***ANXIETY.***

Down You stretched to this lowly **outcast.**
When I call out Your name, the demons *shriek.*
You remember no more my ugly **past**,
This grateful leper remains at Your *feet.*

With Christ in Me, I live in splendid **light**,
Father's calling, my heritage is *traced.*
Been set free from the darkness, fear no **plight**.
My confidence in You is not *misplaced.*

Whenever I'm asked how I know You **CARE**,
My answer is because You made me Your **heir**!

LtA

Notes:

But God demonstrates His own love toward us, in that while we were still sinners, Christ died for us.

Romans 5:8 | NKJV

Remarkable Love

Newness of life, Your love **manifested,**
DEMONSTRATING Your love, no room for ***doubt.***
Your clear evidence cannot be **tested.**
Hidden no longer, no other way ***out.***

In our stead, You saved from eternal **death,**
Your elect polluted, You took our ***place.***
Dying on a cross, You drew Your last **breath.**
On my own, dead in sin, I had no ***case.***

No longer parted for **eternity,**
pardoned, renewed, no longer a ***stranger.***
Made me righteous through our **paternity,**
Yahweh's redeeming plan not in ***danger.***

You liberated the SINNER and **DIED,**
falling short, with Your help, I won't **backslide.**

LHA

Notes:

*I stand silently to listen for the
one I love,
waiting as long as it takes for the
Lord to rescue me.
For God alone has become my
Savior.*

Psalm 62:1 | TPT

Holy Time

You can dispose of my life as You **please**.
During the fight, my faith becomes *fragile*.
When I cannot STAND, I sink to my **knees**.
Life's many twists and turns makes me *agile*.

Nothing in myself in which to *rely,*
I've tested my assets, GOD is **ample**.
My means of reliance, You do *supply*.
Power to defeat, my foes won't **trample**.

Given dispensations of **providence**,
Spirit calm, soul SILENT—in *harmony*.
I patiently expect **deliverance**,
thankful, eyeing my SAVIOR'S *armory*.

WAITING strengthens me to ward off **darkness**.
In the end, my enemy looks **harmless**.

LHA

Notes:

The gatekeeper opens the gate for him, and the sheep recognize his voice and come to him. He calls his own sheep by name and leads them out. ⁴ After he has gathered his own flock, he walks ahead of them, and they follow him because they know his voice. ⁵ They won't follow a stranger; they will run from him because they don't know his voice.

John 10:3-5 | NLT

Doorkeeper

Called, You OPENED the door of faith for **all**.
Great Shepherd enables my heart to ***hear***.
In the beginning, there was a great **fall**.
Living Water flows, never stale, we ***cheer***.

Christian holiness, the path You will **guide**.
Example of the Gospel, Bread of ***Life***.
LEADS away from danger, no need to **hide**,
A STRANGER I won't follow, would cause ***strife***.

Pursuing Your ways for You do **endear**,
You whisper soft, so I press in ***closer***.
While I FOLLOW, I will offer my **ear**,
so I hear the VOICE of The ***Composer***.

Point the way, practical, safe; love You **lend**,
when the thief and robber come, You **defend**.

Notes:

So God created man in His own image; in the image of God He created him; male and female He created them.

Genesis 1:27 | NKJV

New Creation

Adam was CREATED first, out of **earth.**
Eve from his side, GOD loudly *broadcasting,*
servants of this world, replenish, give **birth!**
Delight in your birthright *everlasting*.

On the sixth day, made last of all **creatures.**
Before them, creation to *contemplate.*
Allied to both worlds, His novel **preachers**.
Spirit resembling God, cannot *debate.*

Flesh, spirit, heaven, and earth came **together.**
Conform to Your will, there's no *contender*.
God's agents on earth, storms we will **weather**.
Body and mind submissive to Your *splendor.*

From one common stock, we find ourselves **linked,**
to love and assist, making us **distinct**.

LHA

Notes:

If any of you lacks wisdom, you should ask God, who gives generously to all without finding fault, and it will be given to you.

James 1:5 | NIV

Divine Teaching

WISDOM and grace, an eternal **fountain.**
Please, Teacher, assist me to bear the ***trials.***
Discern lessons You teach up this **mountain,**
new duties that grow from them transmits ***smiles.***

I'll lose the benefit by **complaining.**
Bear my case before You, the gap not ***wide.***
Spirit of rebellion flee, I'm **straining.**
Prone to sin, I need a heavenly ***guide.***

With my confidence of outcome **shaken,**
Divine aid driven by desire, ***rendered,***
My prayers lifted, You have not **forsaken.**
No withholding of favor, ***surrendered.***

Freely receiving kindness, no **reproach.**
Your throne of grace I can always **approach.**

Notes:

I can do all things through him who strengthens me.

Philippians 4:13 | ESV

Consciousness

Domesticated by Your **leadership**,
Son of Man, sin and weakness I *admit*.
I accept God's free grace, a **partnership**.
Exposing my flaws, to Christ I *commit*.

STRENGTH originates from my **Redeemer**.
Whose STRENGTH and wisdom I now have *access*.
You imparted these gifts, I'm no **dreamer**,
to fulfill Your will I can now *progress*.

Inward appearance, fashioned a pure **heart**.
More of You, less of me, patient and *meek*.
Disposition by grace now we can **start**.
My STRENGTH made perfect while I remain *weak*.

The same Spirit Who raised Jesus, my **Lord**,
found a home in me, I carry His **Sword**!

LHA

Notes:

If you then, being evil, know how to give good gifts to your children, how much more will your Father who is in heaven give good things to those who ask Him!

Matthew 7:11 | NKJV

Natural Root

Original sin, ashes for **beauty,**
humankind's depravity, not ***complete.***
Burdens of brokenness, not my **duty.**
Divine love pushing forward, no ***retreat.***

True supplication brings Holy **sonship,**
no greater sense than Your paternal ***love.***
Human nature, yes, but not my **kingship,**
Your creation You will not dispose ***of.***

Blessed endless mercy, grace, and **goodness,**
pure esteem for my FATHER, ***imitate.***
Spiritual GIFTS adds to the **fullness,**
wisdom and insight, come as a ***floodgate.***

Promised One, Your sovereign hand does **bestow,**
the final judgment, dealt to all **below.**

LHA

Notes:

You were cleansed from your sins when you obeyed the truth, so now you must show sincere love to each other as brothers and sisters. Love each other deeply with all your heart.

1 Peter 1:22 | NLT

Brotherly Love

Cannot be pure lacking own **intention.**
God's fountain opened for CLEANSING of *sin.*
Spirit moves me to this **intervention.**
TRUTH, means of sanctification, *begin.*

Heart purified from all earthly **designs.**
Spirit, joined to TRUTH, for world's *redemption.*
Gospel profits minds not on the **sidelines.**
OBEYING the TRUTH, without *exemption.*

Can I profess to follow Christ, His **bride?**
Attaining higher degrees of LOVE the *norm,*
unless I LOVE those for whom Christ has **died?**
An effort I make for God to *conform.*

Christian LOVE in my heart by Your TRUTH **springs,**
Christian LOVE, that follows the King of **Kings.**

LHA

Notes:

Let us then with confidence draw near to the throne of grace, that we may receive mercy and find grace to help in time of need.

Hebrews 4:16 | ESV

Great High Priest

Mercy-seat, the blood of the Lamb **consents,**
I come with boldness looking for ***pardon.***
CONFIDENCE in the sacrifice **presents,**
A place where God and I meet, our ***garden.***

Sufficient gift for my **iniquity**,
Intercede, I need Your MERCY, ***Savior.***
RECEIVING support from the **Trinity**,
Your will, distribute this Divine ***favor.***

THRONE OF GRACE, accessible, I **exhort.**
High Priest has knowledge of what's ***required.***
Favor throughout trials of life, please **support,**
Certain of help before I've ***expired.***

Strange that any should rely on their own **strength**,
When God's available within arm's **length.**

Notes:

If then you were raised with Christ, seek those things which are above, where Christ is, sitting at the right hand of God. ² Set your mind on things above, not on things on the earth.

Colossians 3:1-2 | NKJV

Union

CHRIST gave new life when He RAISED death to **life,**
dead to sin; virtue of *resurrection.*
A lively hope under His *protection.*
Hues unknown, streets of gold—the **afterlife.**

Mere earthly pleasures no longer *allure.*
Fixing affections on heavenly **THINGS**,
pursuing the ABOVE, I will **secure,**
the preparation to dwell with the **King**.

Mind on spiritual, not **transitory.**
No need to worry about the *abyss.*
Thoughts occupied where He is in **glory.**
CHRIST paved the way for unknown *bliss.*

My eternal home completely **furnished,**
this heavenly house I seek in **earnest.**

LtA

Notes:

But you are not like that, for you are a chosen people. You are royal priests, a holy nation, God's very own possession. As a result, you can show others the goodness of God, for he called you out of the darkness into his wonderful light.

1 Peter 2:9 |NLT

Elected

CHOSEN, blood bought, redeemed, and **distinguished**.
Belonging, secured, as His ***possession,***
our bond with the King never **relinquished**.
Exhibit holy life, the ***impression.***

Consecrated and accepted by **God**.
A Kingdom offering ***sacrifices***.
DARKNESS: emblem of ignorance **abroad**,
under duty to God, He ***suffices***.

LIGHT: the emblem to contrast the great **change**.
Sin and misery before ***conversion***.
Mind dark, now clear. Christ can **rearrange**.
Exponents to the gospel ***dispersion***.

Privileged to show praise, Him Who has **CALLED**,
proclaiming God's glory, message not **stalled**.

LHA

Notes:

Looking to Jesus, the founder and perfecter of our faith, who for the joy that was set before him endured the cross, despising the shame, and is seated at the right hand of the throne of God.

Hebrews 12:2 | ESV

Race of Faith

Over my FAITH, You preside as **Captain**.
Eyes fixed upon Christ, miraculous *cure*.
Sustainer of FAITH, believer's **wrapped in,**
accomplished objective, You did *procure*.

JOY of delivering all who fall **short,**
showing ENDURING FAITH in the good ***news.***
Obtain the prize in triumph, I **exhort,**
bestowing the promised crown, You will ***choose.***

Glorious rewards of heaven in **reach,**
my Savior willingly bore the ***sorrow.***
Hung in SHAME on a CROSS for all to **teach,**
disgrace to eternal glory, ***morrow.***

Your presence the point the race will **finish,**
SEATED on high, glory won't **diminish.**

LHA

Notes:

Do you not know?
Have you not heard?
The Lord is the everlasting God,
the Creator of the ends of the earth.
He will not grow tired or weary,
and his understanding no one can fathom.
²⁹ He gives strength to the weary and increases the power of the weak.

Isaiah 40:28-29 |NIV

Confidence in God

Recall the knowledge of Your **character.**
Remember Your dealings of ***faithfulness.***
Assurances I'm Your **inheritor,**
unchangeable, Your purposes ***progress.***

God's providence is not some mere **theory.**
The Lord will not neglect His ***creation.***
You formed the EARTH, did not become **WEARY,**
not TIRED, able to guard Your ***nation.***

Boundless skill found in the works of Your **hands.**
Wisdom unexplained; I wish You could ***share.***
Aware of the needs of those in Your **land,**
ruler of the universe does not ***err.***

Much unsearchable and **mysterious,**
eternal power not **imperious.**

LHA

Notes:

The Lord is good,
A stronghold in the day of trou-
ble;
And He knows those who
trust in Him.

Nahum 1:7 | NKJV

He Knows

Full of mercy and sweetness, GOOD and **mighty**;
    Himself imparting kindness to His ***own,***
    never overlooked by the **Almighty.**
The LORD approves and preserves who is ***known***.

    Trust as Rahab, when Jericho **perished.**
    Take refuge in You, no place of ***escape.***
    Consistent, persistent faith is **cherished.**
    TRUST with a reward leaving mouths ***agape.***

    He KNOWS each, a knowledge ever-**present.**
    Among the wrath, You vow Divine ***blessing.***
    Those who defy and choose not to **repent,**
    Your response to those unknown, ***distressing.***

    Like Nineveh, wrath used for **enemies**.
    Who TRUSTS in the LORD, Divine **legacies.**

LHA

Notes:

I have told you these things, so that in me you may have peace. In this world you will have trouble. But take heart! I have overcome the world.

John 16:33 | NIV

Victory

True PEACE found in Christ, no fabled **stories.**
Assured triumph over our *enemy.*
Son of Man revealing heaven's **glories,**
Satan, humbled foe, his *identity.*

Plunged into tribulations don't ask **why.**
Downcast, no! Jesus, our great *exchanger,*
exposed to TROUBLE does not **terrify,**
under His banner beyond all *danger.*

Clothed in God's armor, benefits **rendered.**
Unity with God gives peace *unending.*
Following the victor's train, **surrendered.**
The cure of distress before *ascending.*

Satan exploits as he lays the next **snare,**
but he is the one who needs to **beware.**

LHA

Notes:

CONCLUSION

The heavens declare the glory of God, and the sky above proclaims his handiwork. ² Day to day pours out speech, and night to night reveals knowledge. ³ There is no speech, nor are there words, whose voice is not heard. ⁴ Their voice goes out through all the earth, and their words to the end of the world. In them he has set a tent for the sun, ⁵ which comes out like a bridegroom leaving his chamber, and, like a strong man, runs its course with joy. ⁶ Its rising is from the end of the heavens, and its circuit to the end of them, and there is nothing hidden from its heat. ⁷ The law of the LORD is perfect reviving the soul; the testimony of the LORD is sure, making wise the simple; ⁸ the precepts of the LORD are right, rejoicing the heart; the commandment of the LORD is pure, enlightening the eyes; ⁹ the fear of the LORD is clean, enduring forever; the rules of the LORD are true, and righteous altogether. ¹⁰ More to be desired are they than gold, even much fine gold; sweeter also than honey and drippings of the honeycomb. ¹¹ Moreover, by them is your servant warned; in keeping them there is great reward. ¹² Who can discern his errors? Declare me innocent from hidden faults. ¹³ Keep back your servant also from presumptuous sins; let them not have dominion over me! Then I shall be blameless, and innocent of great transgression. ¹⁴ Let the words of my mouth and the meditation of my heart be acceptable in your sight,

O Lord, my rock and my redeemer.
Psalm 19 | ESV

Some people don't feel they've ever been loved, or even feel that they are worthy of love. The Truth is: God loves you. You were chosen and His love is eternal and never-ending. His love will fill and satisfy you until you become transformed by it. This devotional is God's love letter to your mind, heart, soul, and body. I pray that you enjoyed your journey through the thirty-one sonnets and had your heart awakened to your Father's love for you.

It is my prayer that the Holy Spirit and this sonnet devotional will help you discover a deeper appreciation of biblical poetry.

Finally, if you find yourself in a position to lead someone to Christ, you are qualified to do so! Jesus is looking at the heart; not an education. Simply tell them your story, no one can dispute or argue with you—it is your story. God uses people to share the Gospel. You don't have to be paid clergy to spread the Word.

> *Whoever wants to be my disciple must deny themselves and take up their cross daily and follow me.* **Luke 9:23 | NIV**

> *If you remain in me and my words remain in you, ask whatever you wish, and it will be done for you. ⁸ This is to my Father's glory, that you bear much fruit, showing yourselves to be my disciples.* **John 15: 7-8 | NIV**

It has been a privilege to serve the Kingdom's purpose for this sonnet devotional. I pray God continues to bless you and yours.

May His grace and peace be with you always,

L&A

ABOUT THE AUTHOR

Christian Life Coaching by LtA is a teaching ministry with a heart for serving others. LtA is a professional Certified Christian Life Coach (CCLC). LtA is a pseudonym for me because all honor and glory go to God, not me. It is my privilege to help anyone address worldly struggles using eternal strategies. It's an honor to help bring hurting people to a place of rest through reliance on Jesus Christ.

> *But he said to me, 'My grace is sufficient for you, for my power is made perfect in weakness.' Therefore, I will boast all the more gladly about my weaknesses, so that Christ's power may rest on me.* **2 Corinthians 12:9**

Christian Life Coaching by LtA suggests tools for positive change in teaching methods rather than only affirmation. I pray you take refuge in the pages and obtain comfort, encouragement, and a renewed sense of worth.

Affirmation sells; affirmation does not serve in transformative change. It is only upon applying the Truth to our lives that we are able to see tangible transformation. If you're one of these people who are hoping for another book of affirmation, I pray you will invest in yourself. Continue reading and studying God's Word and books that challenge you, not just tell you what your flesh wants to hear. Know that I love you in God's love. Know that I sympathize with you. Know that I understand why you may have a limited perspective if you are a part-time Christian fighting a full time enemy. Our world is full of "spiritual leaders" who are willing and eager to tell you what you want to hear. Who doesn't want to be affirmed? Who doesn't want to feel good? Many have chosen to put their trust in these men and women only to come to the realization that something is missing. If you are one of these people, God is calling you to go deeper with Him.

LtA feels called to express God's Word in a way for people to grow in their maturity in Christ and feel conviction, never condemnation. My prayer is that you allow God's Word to minister as revelation to your heart as well as knowledge for your mind.

LtA teaches on a number of topics, with a particular focus on purposeful living which involves teaching how to love and live on God's Word.

Through Christian Life Coaching by LtA's teachings and resources, and by combining honesty and vulnerability with God's Word, God has provided Christian Life Coaching by LtA opportunities to meet the needs of the suffering and bring the Gospel in a practical way. Christian Life Coaching by LtA is able to reach a worldwide audience through publications, social media, and the internet.

Christian Life Coaching by LtA's particular outreach passion is targeted to reaching the lost and hurting with the love of Christ. Over the years, God has provided Christian Life Coaching by LtA with many opportunities to share testimonies and the life-changing message of the Gospel. Having suffered abuse, as well as just dealing with the struggles of everyday life, LtA discovered the freedom to live victoriously by applying God's Word to everyday life and in turn desires to help others do the same.

LtA is and continues to be an incredible testimony of the dynamic, redeeming work of Jesus Christ.

It is not my calling to fill your ears with frivolous words that have temporal and non-lasting transformative effect. Transformation is a daily activity that we actively participate in with the Holy Spirit. The transformation and our testimony is powerful and affirming of our faith, as we enter the world on a daily basis. God loves us all and calls us His, but we also have the privilege of being His witnesses to a fallen world. As children of God, if we act, talk, and live like everyone else, we are not honoring our part of being Christ's Ambassadors. I pray you will see the pages as tools to lift you to new levels and help lift others. It is my calling and passion to help you live your best life and help prepare you for eternal life in Heaven. I am grateful for the opportunity to serve all who read these pages.

God bless, LtA

ABOUT KHARIS PUBLISHING

KHARIS PUBLISHING is an independent, traditional publishing house with a core mission to publish impactful books, and channel proceeds into establishing mini-libraries or resource centers for orphanages in developing countries, so these kids will learn to read, dream, and grow. Every time you purchase a book from Kharis Publishing or partner as an author, you are helping give these kids an amazing opportunity to read, dream, and grow. Kharis Publishing is an imprint of Kharis Media LLC. Learn more at https://www.kharispublishing.com.

www.ingramcontent.com/pod-product-compliance
Lightning Source LLC
Chambersburg PA
CBHW070158100426
42743CB00013B/2959